THE VERY BEST OF
ADELE
FOR UKULELE

WISE PUBLICATIONS
part of The Music Sales Group
London / New York / Paris / Sydney / Copenhagen /
Berlin / Madrid / Hong Kong / Tokyo

T0039686

Published by
Wise Publications
14-15 Berners Street,
London W1T 3LJ, UK.

Exclusive Distributors:
Music Sales Limited
Distribution Centre, Newmarket Road,
Bury St Edmunds, Suffolk IP33 3YB, UK.
Music Sales Pty Limited
20 Resolution Drive, Caringbah, NSW 2229, Australia.

Order No. AM1004487
ISBN: 978-1-78038-475-7
This book © Copyright 2011 Wise Publications,
a division of Music Sales Limited.

Edited by Adrian Hopkins.
Produced by shedwork.com
Cover designed by Tim Field.

Printed in the EU.

Your Guarantee of Quality:

As publishers, we strive to produce every book
to the highest commercial standards.

This book has been carefully designed
to minimise awkward page turns and
to make playing from it a real pleasure.

Particular care has been given to specifying acid-free,
neutral-sized paper made from pulps which have
not been elemental chlorine bleached.

This pulp is from farmed sustainable forests and
was produced with special regard for the environment.

Throughout, the printing and binding have been
planned to ensure a sturdy, attractive publication
which should give years of enjoyment.

If your copy fails to meet our high standards,
please inform us and we will gladly replace it.

www.musicsales.com

Chasing Pavements

Words & Music by Adele Adkins & Eg White

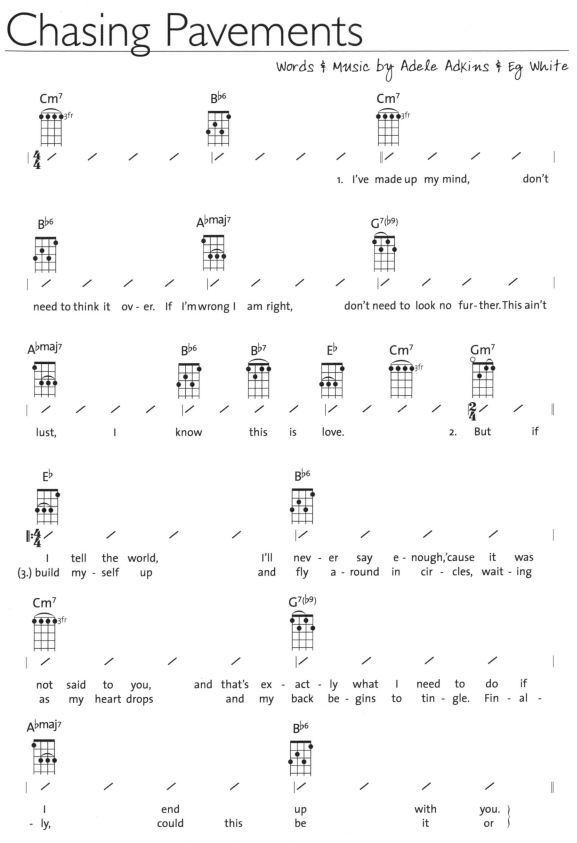

1. I've made up my mind, don't need to think it ov - er. If I'm wrong I am right, don't need to look no fur - ther. This ain't lust, I know this is love. 2. But if

I tell the world,
(3.) build my - self up

I'll nev - er say e - nough, 'cause it was
and fly a - round in cir - cles, wait - ing

not said to you, and that's ex - act - ly what I need to do if
as my heart drops and my back be - gins to tin - gle. Fin - al -

I
- ly,

end
could

this

up
be

with
it

you.
or

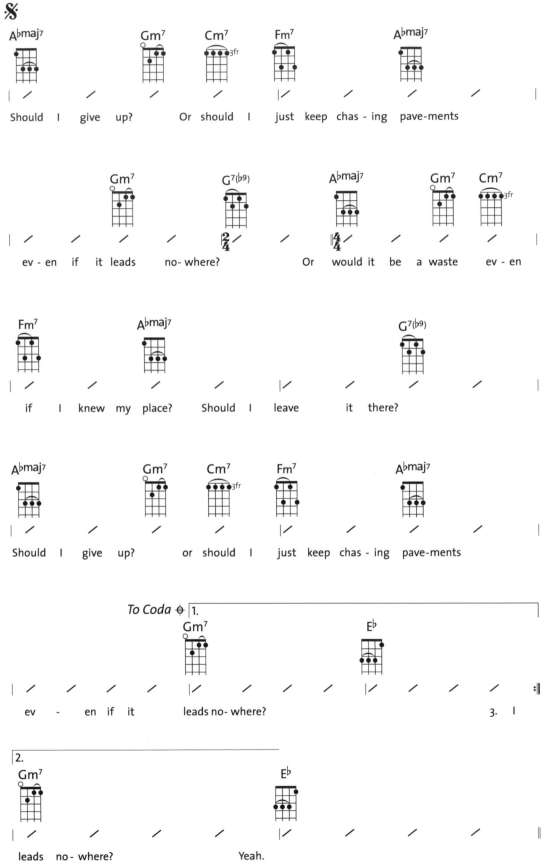

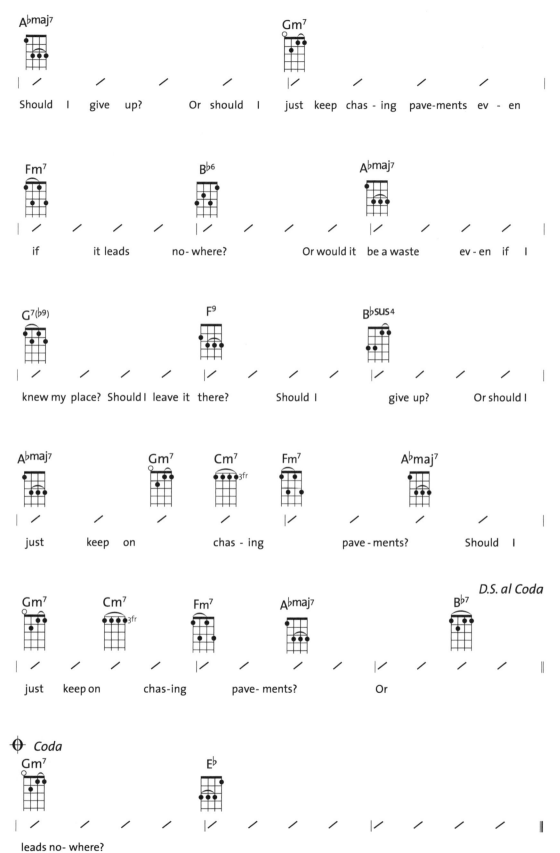

A♭maj7

Gm7

Should I give up? Or should I just keep chas - ing pave-ments ev - en

Fm7

B♭6

A♭maj7

if it leads no- where? Or would it be a waste ev - en if I

G7(♭9)

F9

B♭sus4

knew my place? Should I leave it there? Should I give up? Or should I

A♭maj7

Gm7 Cm7

Fm7

A♭maj7

just keep on chas - ing pave - ments? Should I

Gm7 Cm7

Fm7

A♭maj7

D.S. al Coda

B♭7

just keep on chas-ing pave- ments? Or

⊕ *Coda*

Gm7

E♭

leads no- where?

Cold Shoulder

Words & Music by Adele Adkins

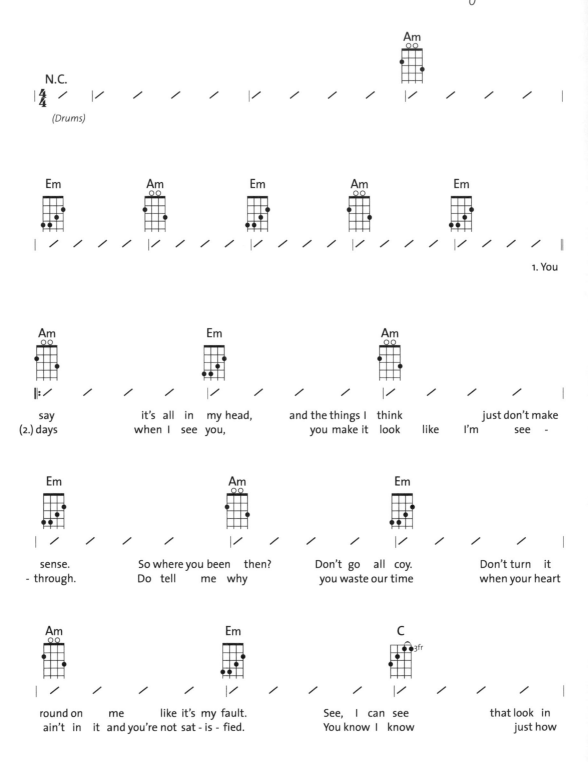

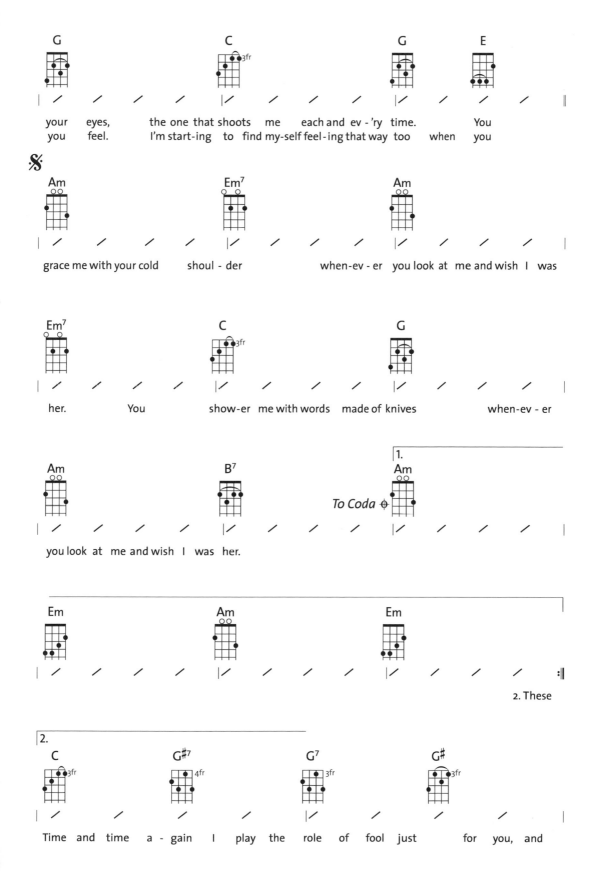

G   C   G   E

your eyes,   the one that shoots me   each and ev - 'ry time.   You
you feel.   I'm start-ing to find my-self feel-ing that way too   when   you

Am   Em⁷   Am

grace me with your cold   shoul - der   when-ev - er you look at me and wish I was

Em⁷   C   G

her.   You   show-er me with words   made of knives   when-ev - er

Am   B⁷   1.   Am

To Coda ⊕

you look at me and wish I was her.

Em   Am   Em

2. These

2.

C   G♯⁷   G⁷   G♯

Time and time a - gain I play the role of fool just   for you, and

7

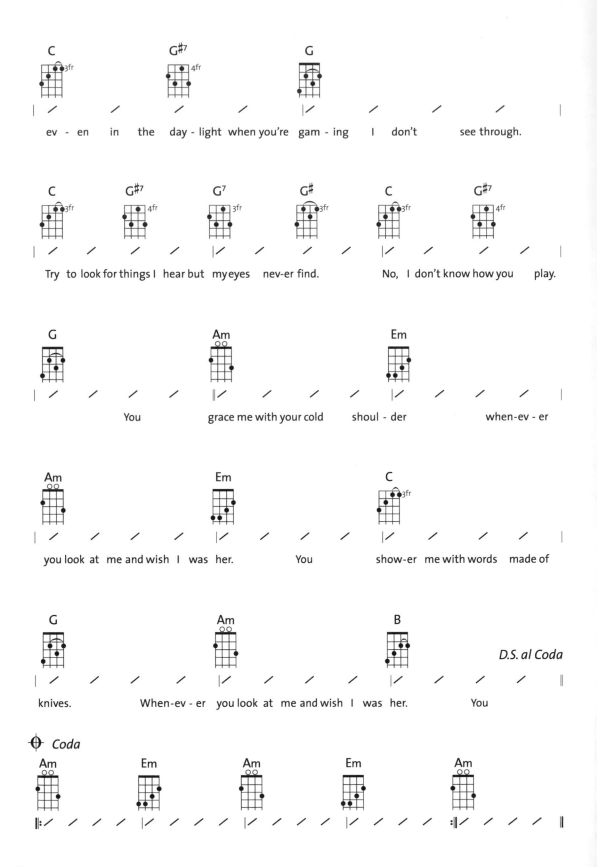

C   G#7   G

ev - en   in   the   day - light when you're gam - ing   I   don't   see through.

C   G#7   G7   G#   C   G#7

Try to look for things I hear but my eyes nev-er find.   No, I don't know how you   play.

G   Am   Em

You   grace me with your cold   shoul - der   when-ev - er

Am   Em   C

you look at me and wish I was her.   You   show-er me with words   made of

G   Am   B

D.S. al Coda

knives.   When-ev - er you look at me and wish I was her.   You

⊕ *Coda*

Am   Em   Am   Em   Am

Crazy For You

Words & Music by Adele Adkins

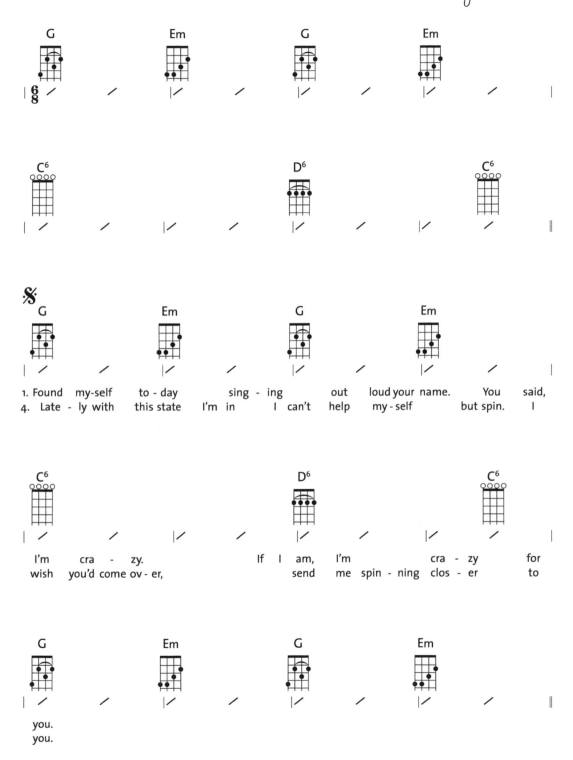

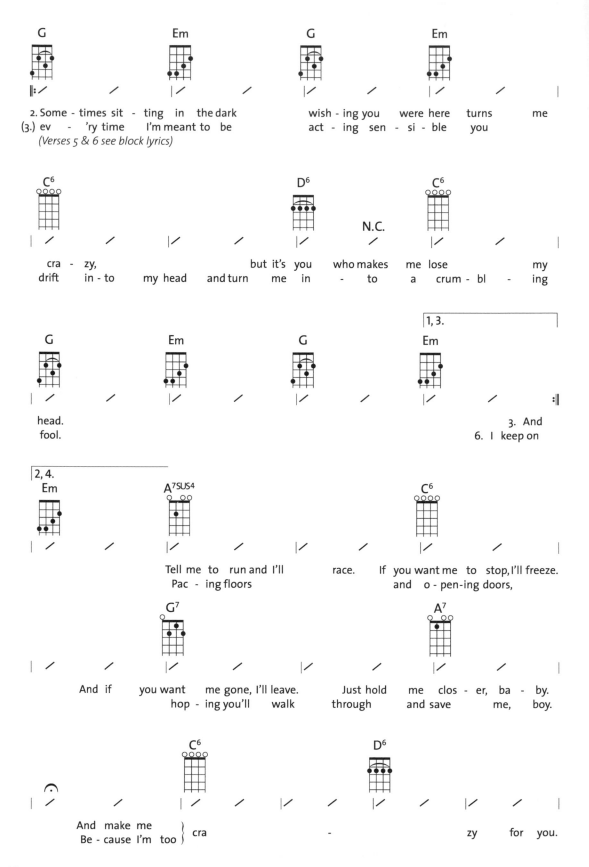

G   **Em**   **G**   **Em**

2. Some - times sit - ting in the dark   wish - ing you were here turns me
(3.) ev - 'ry time I'm meant to be   act - ing sen - si - ble you

(Verses 5 & 6 see block lyrics)

C⁶   **D⁶**   **N.C.**   **C⁶**

cra - zy,   but it's you who makes me lose my
drift in - to my head and turn me in - to a crum - bl - ing

1, 3.

G   **Em**   **G**   **Em**

head.   3. And
fool.   6. I keep on

2, 4.

Em   **A⁷ˢᵁˢ⁴**   **C⁶**

Tell me to run and I'll race. If you want me to stop, I'll freeze.
Pac - ing floors   and o - pen-ing doors,

G⁷   **A⁷**

And if you want me gone, I'll leave. Just hold me clos - er, ba - by.
hop - ing you'll walk through and save me, boy.

C⁶   **D⁶**

And make me } cra - zy for you.
Be - cause I'm too }

10

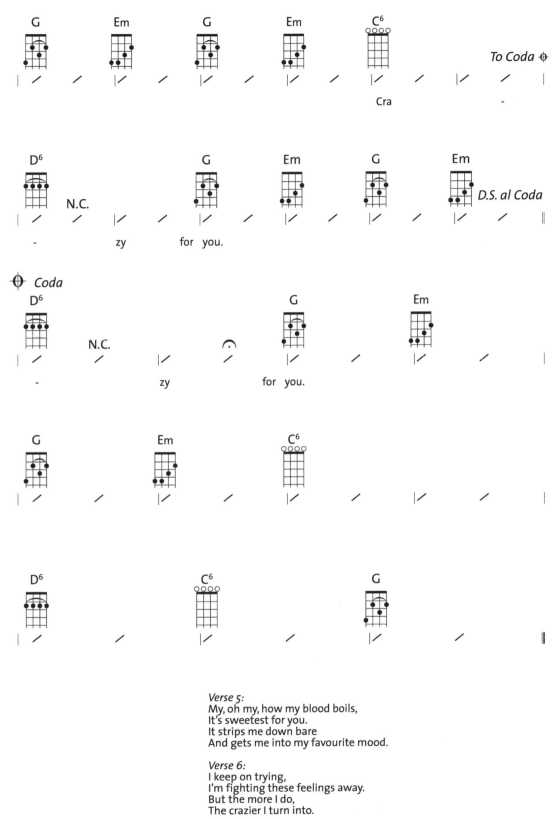

Daydreamer

Words & Music by Adele Adkins

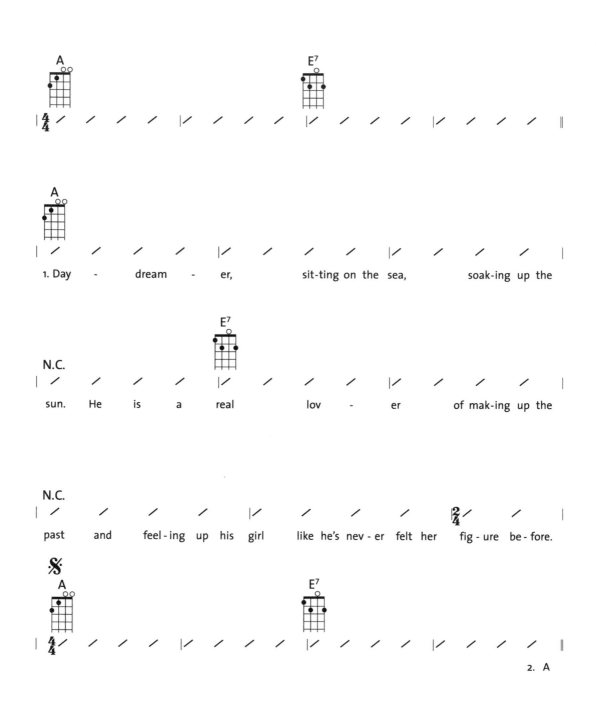

1. Day - dream - er, sit-ting on the sea, soak-ing up the

sun. He is a real lov - er of mak-ing up the

past and feel-ing up his girl like he's nev - er felt her fig - ure be - fore.

2. A

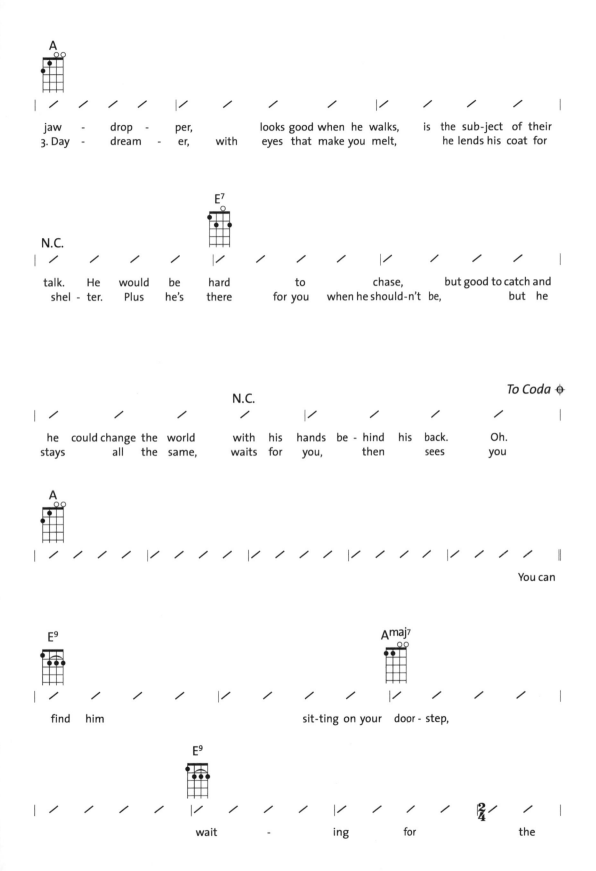

A

| / / / / | / / / / | / / / / |

jaw - drop - per,　　　looks good when he walks,　　is the sub-ject of their
3. Day - dream - er,　　with　eyes that make you melt,　　he lends his coat for

E7

N.C.

| / / / / | / / / / | / / / / |

talk. He would be　hard　　to　　chase,　　but good to catch and
shel - ter. Plus he's there　for you　when he should-n't be,　　but he

To Coda ⊕

N.C.

| / / / / | / / / / | / / |

he could change the world　with his hands be - hind his back.　Oh.
stays　　all the same,　waits for you,　then　sees　you

A

| / / / / | / / / / | / / / / | / / / / | / / / / ‖

You can

E9　　　　　　　　　　　　　　　　　　　Amaj7

| / / / / | / / / / | / / / / |

find him　　　　　　　sit-ting on your door - step,

E9

| / / / / | / / / / | / / ²/₄ / / |

wait　-　ing　for　the

13

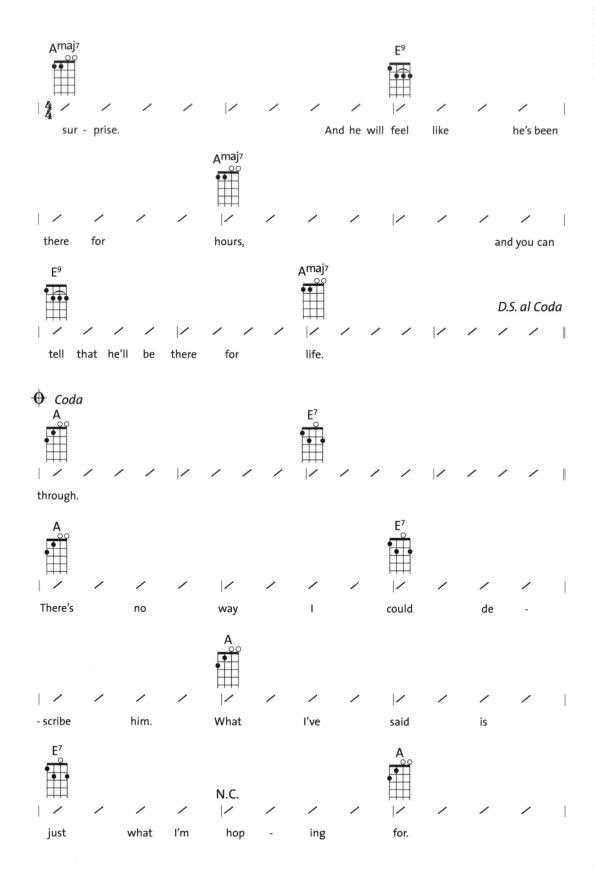

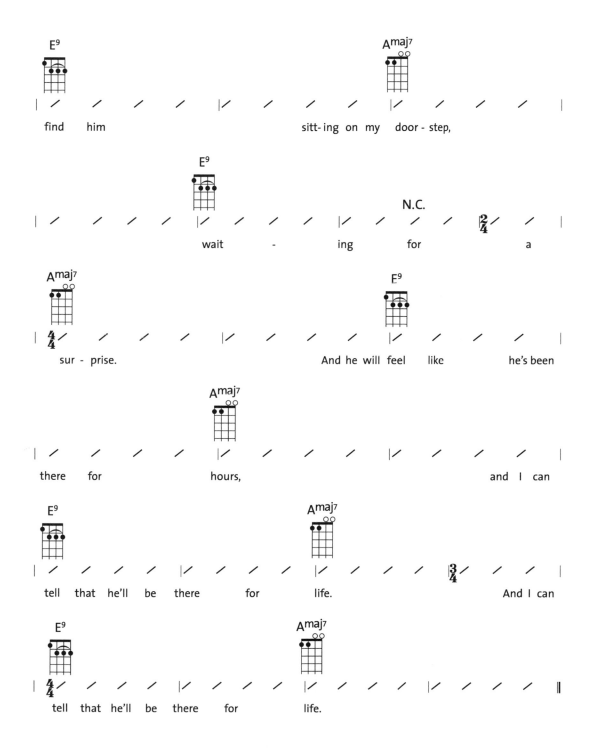

But I will

E⁹   Aᵐᵃʲ⁷

find   him   sitt-ing on my   door - step,

E⁹

wait   -   ing   for   N.C.   a

Aᵐᵃʲ⁷   E⁹

sur - prise.   And he will feel   like   he's been

Aᵐᵃʲ⁷

there   for   hours,   and I can

E⁹   Aᵐᵃʲ⁷

tell   that   he'll   be   there   for   life.   And I can

E⁹   Aᵐᵃʲ⁷

tell   that   he'll   be   there   for   life.

Don't You Remember

Words & Music by Daniel Wilson & Adele Adkins

1. When will I see you a-gain? You left with no good - bye. Not a sin - gle word was said. No fi - nal kiss to seal an - y sins. I had no i - dea of the state we were in.

2. When was the last time that you thought of me? Or have you com- plete - ly e - rased me from your mem - o - ry? I of-ten think a - bout where I went wrong. The more I do the less I know.

(But) I know I have a fick - le heart and a bit - ter - ness. And a

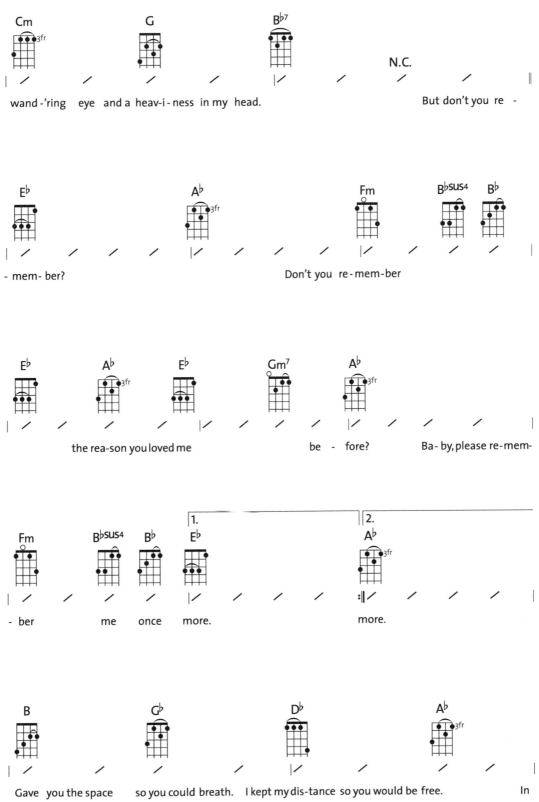

wand-'ring eye and a heav-i-ness in my head. But don't you re -

- mem- ber? Don't you re-mem-ber

the rea-son you loved me be - fore? Ba- by, please re-mem-

- ber me once more. more.

Gave you the space so you could breath. I kept my dis-tance so you would be free. In

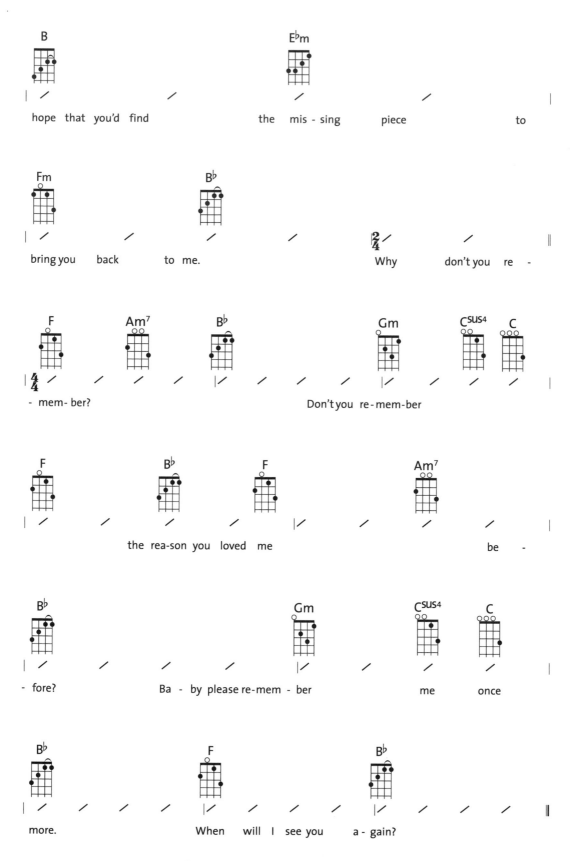

B   E♭m

/   /   /   /

hope that you'd find   the mis - sing   piece   to

Fm   B♭

/   /   /   /   **2/4** /   /

bring you back to me.   Why   don't you re -

F   Am⁷   B♭   Gm   Csus4 C

4/4 / / / / / / / / / / / /

- mem- ber?   Don't you re-mem-ber

F   B♭   F   Am⁷

/   /   /   /   /   /   /   /

the rea-son you loved me   be -

B♭   Gm   Csus4   C

/   /   /   /   /   /   /   /

- fore?   Ba - by please re-mem - ber   me   once

B♭   F   B♭

/   /   /   /   /   /   /   /   /   /   /   /

more.   When will I see you a - gain?

Lovesong

Words by Robert Smith
Music by Robert Smith, Simon Gallup, Laurence Tolhurst,
Porl Thompson, Boris Williams & Roger O'Donnell

1. When-ev-er I'm a-lone with you
2. When-ev-er I'm a-lone with you

you make me feel like I am home a-gain.
you make me feel like I am young a-gain.

When-ev-er I'm a-lone with you
When-ev-er I'm a-lone with you

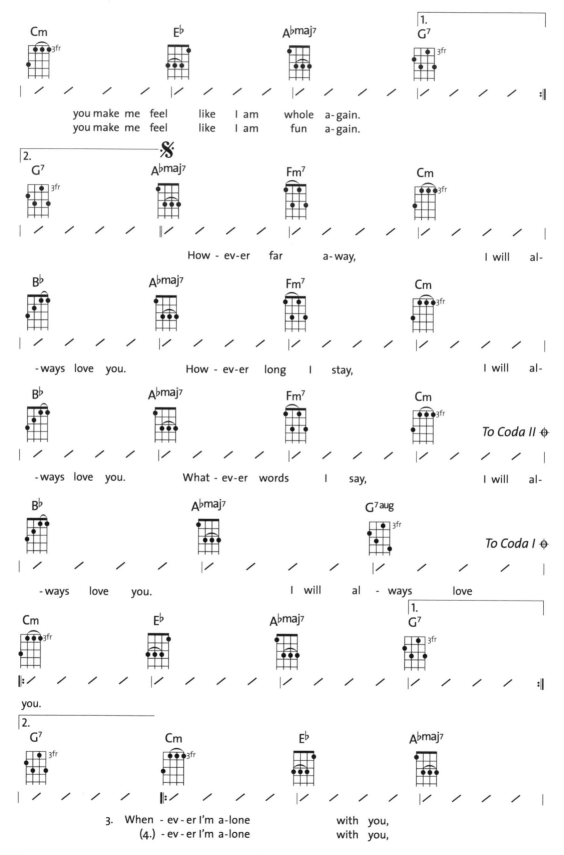

you make me feel like I am whole a-gain.
you make me feel like I am fun a-gain.

How - ev - er far a-way, I will al-

-ways love you. How - ev - er long I stay, I will al-

-ways love you. What - ev - er words I say, I will al-

To Coda II

To Coda I

-ways love you. I will al - ways love

you.

3. When - ev - er I'm a-lone with you,
(4.) - ev - er I'm a-lone with you,

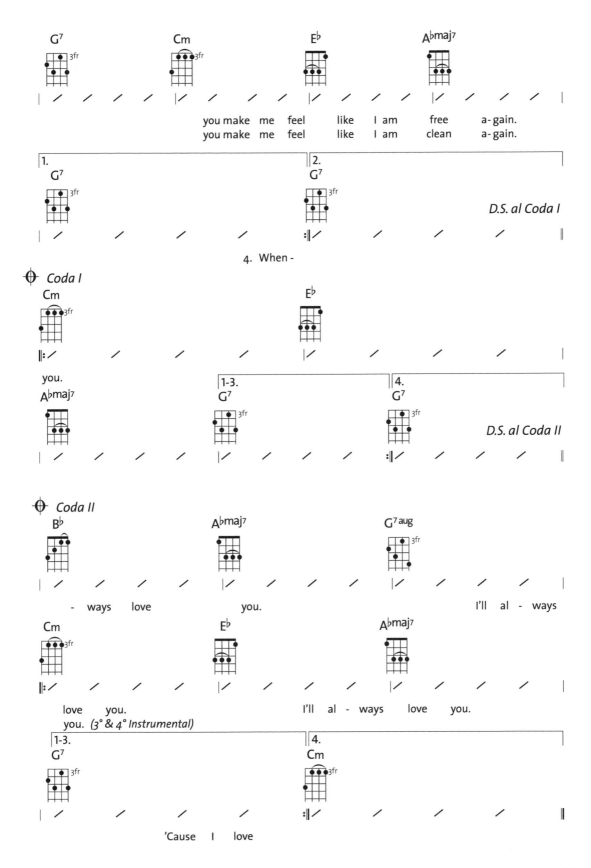

you make me feel like I am free a-gain.
you make me feel like I am clean a-gain.

1.
G⁷

2.
G⁷

D.S. al Coda I

4. When -

Coda I
Cm   E♭

you.
A♭maj7

1-3.
G⁷

4.
G⁷

D.S. al Coda II

Coda II
B♭   A♭maj7   G⁷aug

- ways love you.   I'll al - ways

Cm   E♭   A♭maj7

love you.
you. (3° & 4° Instrumental)
I'll al - ways love you.

1-3.
G⁷

4.
Cm

'Cause I love

He Won't Go

Words & Music by Paul Epworth & Adele Adkins

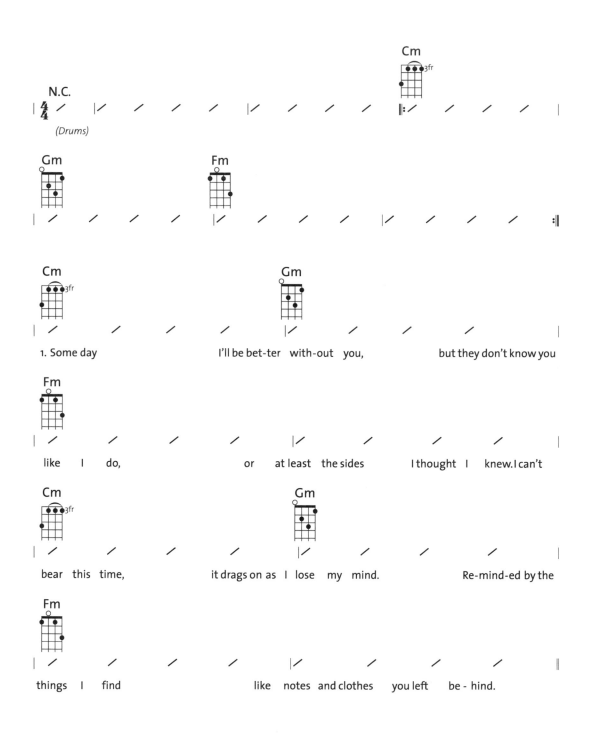

1. Some day I'll be bet-ter with-out you, but they don't know you like I do, or at least the sides I thought I knew. I can't bear this time, it drags on as I lose my mind. Re-mind-ed by the things I find like notes and clothes you left be - hind.

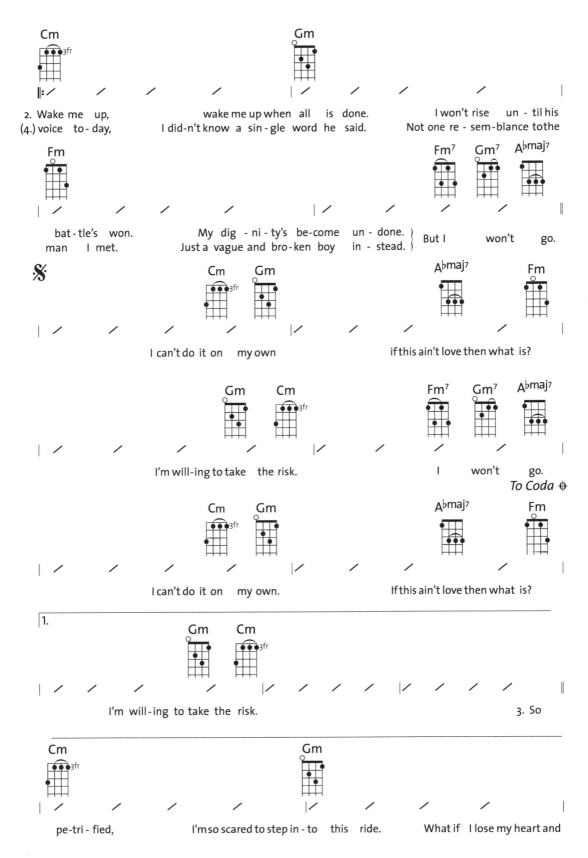

Cm   Gm

2. Wake me up,   wake me up when all   is done.   I won't rise   un - til his
(4.) voice to - day, I did-n't know a sin-gle word he said.   Not one re - sem-blance to the

Fm   Fm⁷   Gm⁷   A♭maj⁷

bat - tle's won.   My dig - ni - ty's be-come un - done. ⎫ But I   won't   go.
man   I met.   Just a vague and bro-ken boy   in - stead. ⎭

𝄋   Cm   Gm   A♭maj⁷   Fm

I can't do it on   my own   if this ain't love then what is?

Gm   Cm   Fm⁷   Gm⁷   A♭maj⁷

I'm will-ing to take   the risk.   I   won't   go.
                                                              To Coda ⊕

Cm   Gm   A♭maj⁷   Fm

I can't do it on   my own.   If this ain't love then what is?

1.
Gm   Cm

I'm will-ing to take the risk.   3. So

Cm   Gm

pe-tri-fied,   I'm so scared to step in-to   this ride.   What if I lose my heart and

23

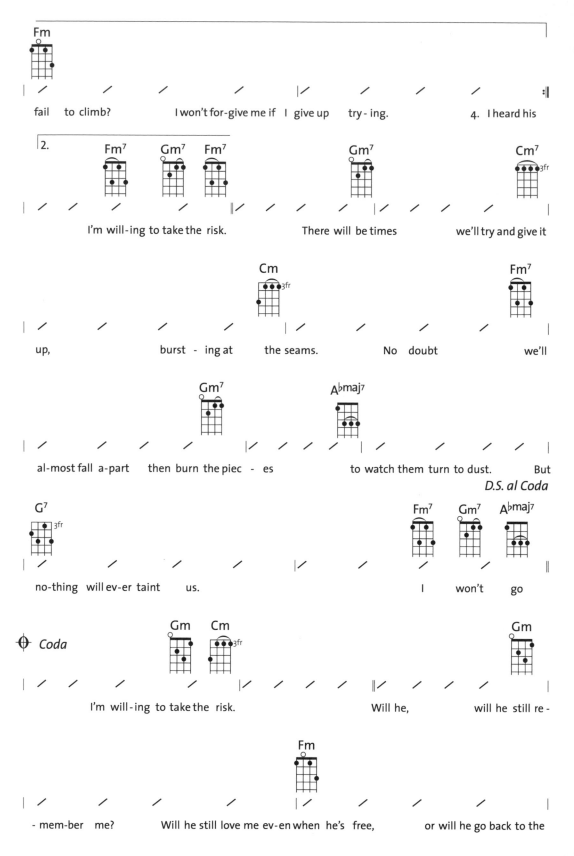

Fm

| / / / / | / / / / :‖

fail   to climb?   I won't for-give me if I give up   try - ing.   4. I heard his

2.   **Fm⁷   Gm⁷ Fm⁷**   **Gm⁷**   **Cm⁷**

| / / / / ‖ / / / / | / / / / |

I'm will-ing to take the risk.   There will be times   we'll try and give it

Cm   **Fm⁷**

| / / / / | / / / / |

up,   burst - ing at   the seams.   No   doubt   we'll

Gm⁷   **A♭maj⁷**

| / / / / | / / / / | / / / / |

al-most fall a-part   then burn the piec - es   to watch them turn to dust.   But

D.S. al Coda

G⁷   **Fm⁷   Gm⁷ A♭maj⁷**

| / / / | / / / / ‖

no-thing will ev-er taint   us.   I   won't   go

⊕ *Coda*   **Gm   Cm**   **Gm**

| / / / / | / / / / ‖ / / / / |

I'm will-ing to take the risk.   Will he,   will he still re -

Fm

| / / / / | / / / / |

- mem-ber me?   Will he still love me ev-en when he's free,   or will he go back to the

24

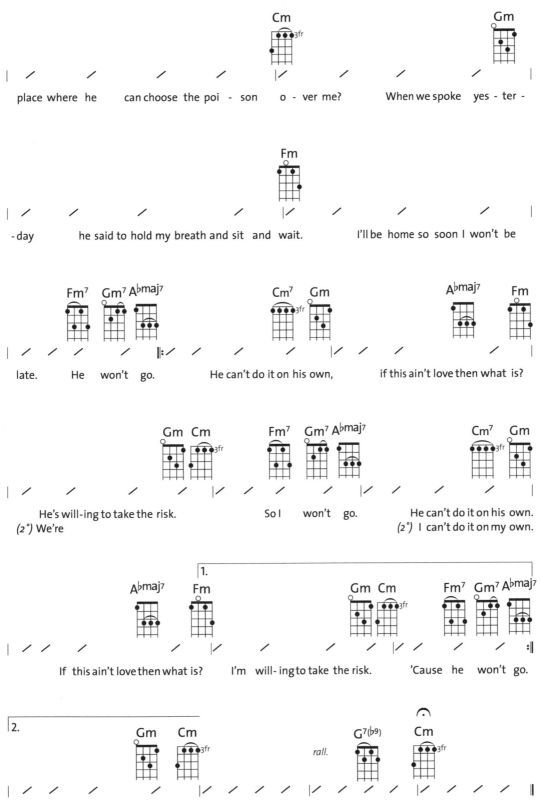

place where he can choose the poi - son o - ver me? When we spoke yes - ter -

-day he said to hold my breath and sit and wait. I'll be home so soon I won't be

late. He won't go. He can't do it on his own, if this ain't love then what is?

He's will-ing to take the risk. So I won't go. He can't do it on his own.
(2°) We're (2°) I can't do it on my own.

1.
If this ain't love then what is? I'm will-ing to take the risk. 'Cause he won't go.

2.
I'm will-ing to take the risk.

Hometown Glory

Words & Music by Adele Adkins

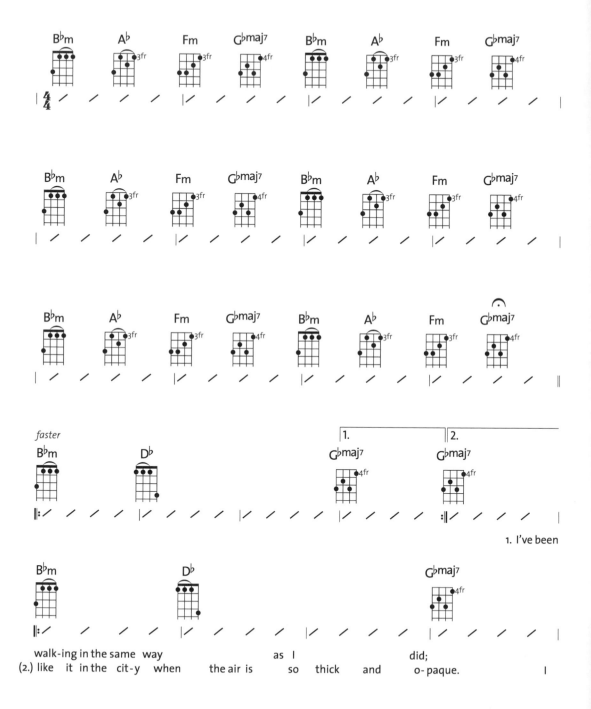

walk-ing in the same way as I did;
(2.) like it in the cit-y when the air is so thick and o-paque. I

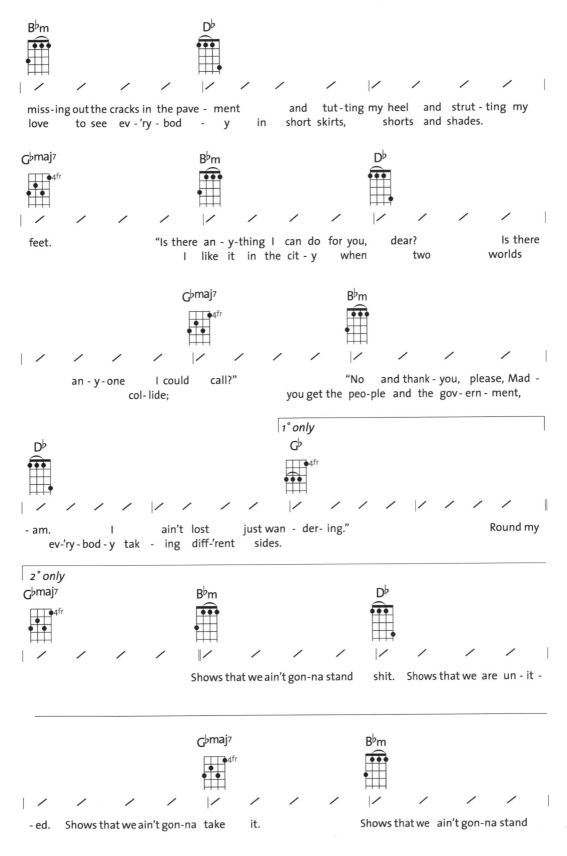

B♭m   D♭

| /   /   /   / |/   /   /   / |/   /   /   / |

miss-ing out the cracks in the pave - ment   and   tut -ting my heel   and strut - ting my
love   to see ev -'ry - bod   -   y   in   short skirts,   shorts and shades.

G♭maj7   B♭m   D♭

| /   /   /   / |/   /   /   / |/   /   /   / |

feet.   "Is there an - y-thing I can do for you,   dear?   Is there
             I   like it   in the cit - y   when   two   worlds

                G♭maj7   B♭m

| /   /   /   / |/   /   /   / |/   /   /   / |

     an - y - one   I could   call?"   "No   and thank - you,   please, Mad -
     col- lide;   you get the peo-ple and the gov - ern - ment,

                                   ⌐ 1° only
   D♭   G♭

| /   /   /   / |/   /   /   / |/   /   /   / ‖

- am.   I   ain't lost   just wan - der- ing."   Round my
     ev-'ry - bod - y tak -   ing diff-'rent   sides.

⌐ 2° only
G♭maj7   B♭m   D♭

| /   /   /   / ‖/   /   /   / |/   /   /   / |

     Shows that we ain't gon-na stand   shit. Shows that we are un - it -

                G♭maj7   B♭m

| /   /   /   / |/   /   /   / |/   /   /   / |

- ed.   Shows that we ain't gon-na take   it.   Shows that we ain't gon-na stand

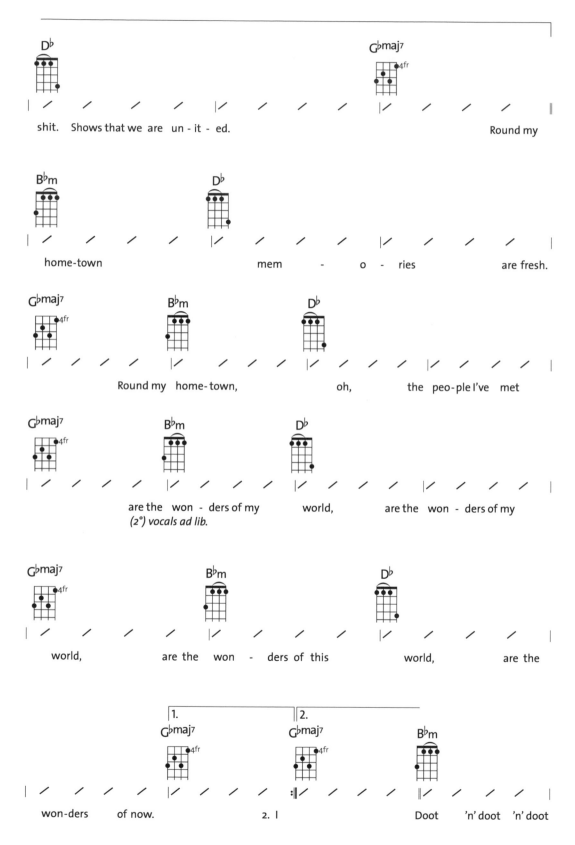

shit. Shows that we are un - it - ed. Round my

home-town mem - o - ries are fresh.

Round my home-town, oh, the peo-ple I've met

are the won - ders of my world, are the won - ders of my
(2°) vocals ad lib.

world, are the won - ders of this world, are the

1.
won-ders of now. 2. I

2.
Doot 'n' doot 'n' doot

28

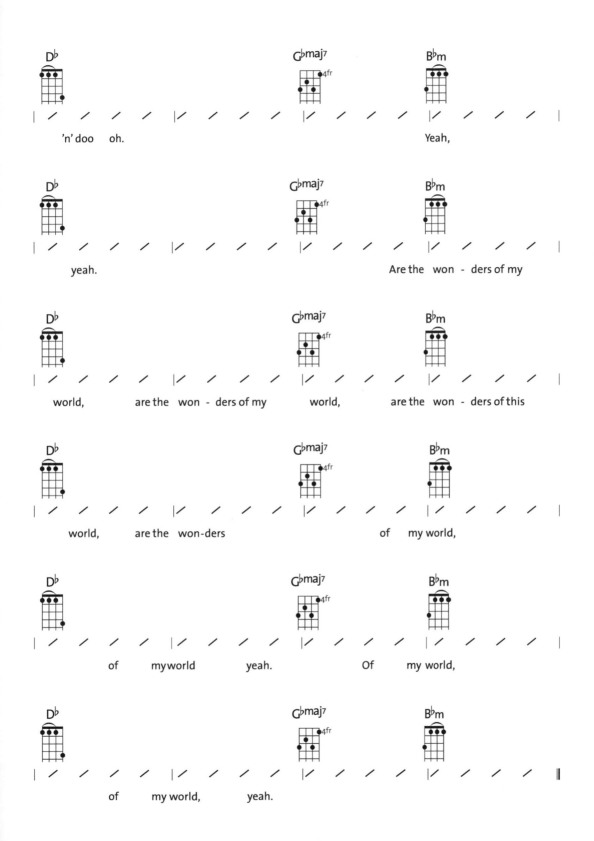

| D♭ | | | | G♭maj7 | | | | B♭m | | | |

'n' doo   oh.   Yeah,

| D♭ | | | | G♭maj7 | | | | B♭m | | | |

yeah.   Are the   won - ders of my

| D♭ | | | | G♭maj7 | | | | B♭m | | | |

world,   are the   won - ders of my   world,   are the   won - ders of this

| D♭ | | | | G♭maj7 | | | | B♭m | | | |

world,   are the   won-ders   of   my world,

| D♭ | | | | G♭maj7 | | | | B♭m | | | |

of   my world   yeah.   Of   my world,

| D♭ | | | | G♭maj7 | | | | B♭m | | | |

of   my world,   yeah.

Make You Feel My Love

Words & Music by Bob Dylan

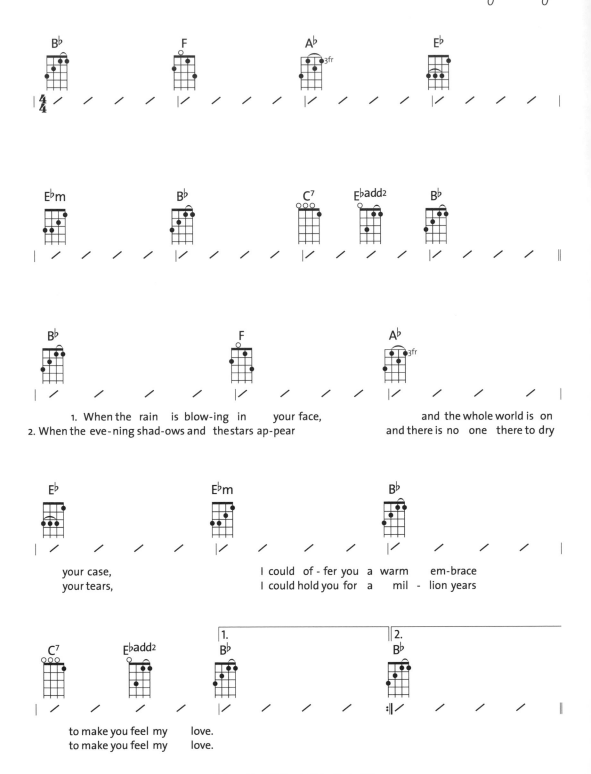

1. When the rain is blow-ing in your face, and the whole world is on
2. When the eve-ning shad-ows and the stars ap-pear and there is no one there to dry

your case, I could of-fer you a warm em-brace
your tears, I could hold you for a mil - lion years

to make you feel my love.
to make you feel my love.

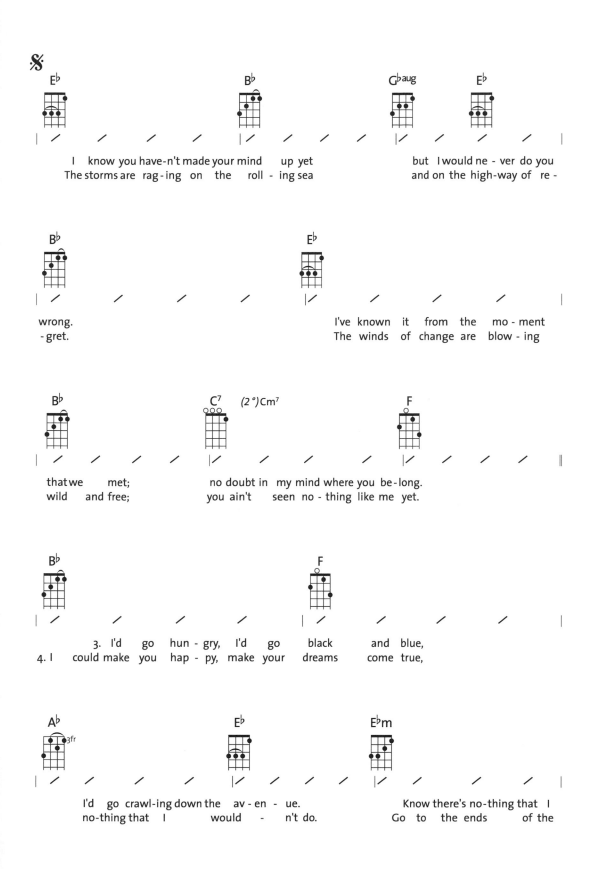

I know you have-n't made your mind   up yet   but I would ne - ver do you
The storms are rag-ing on the   roll - ing sea   and on the high-way of re -

wrong.
- gret.   I've known   it   from   the   mo - ment
                                     The winds   of change are   blow - ing

that we   met;   no doubt in my mind where you be-long.
wild   and free;   you ain't   seen no - thing like me yet.

         3. I'd   go   hun - gry, I'd   go   black   and blue,
4. I   could make you   hap - py, make your   dreams   come true,

I'd   go crawl-ing down the av - en - ue.   Know there's no-thing that I
no-thing that   I   would - n't do.   Go   to the ends   of the

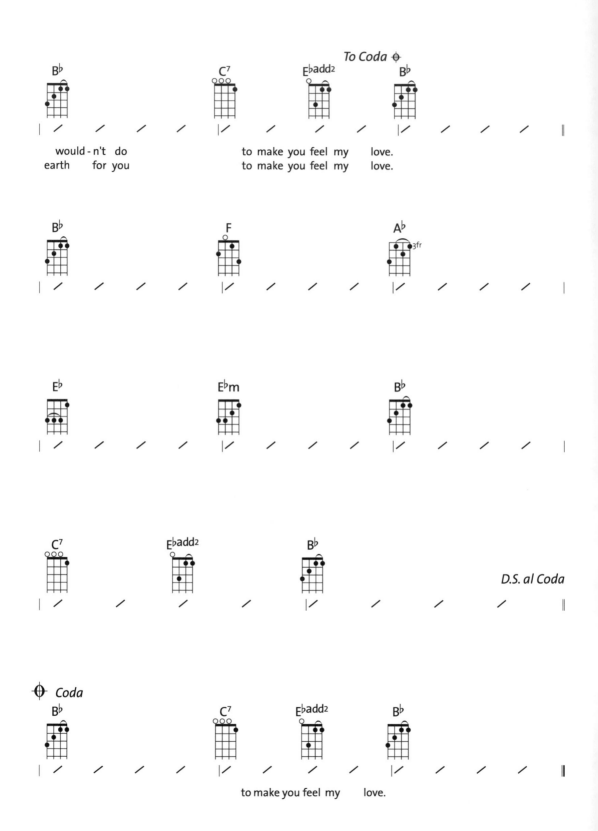

To Coda ⊕

| B♭ | | | | C⁷ | | E♭add2 | | B♭ | | | |

would-n't do   to make you feel my   love.
earth   for you   to make you feel my   love.

D.S. al Coda

⊕ *Coda*

to make you feel my   love.

32

Many Shades Of Black

Words & Music by Jack White & Brendan Benson

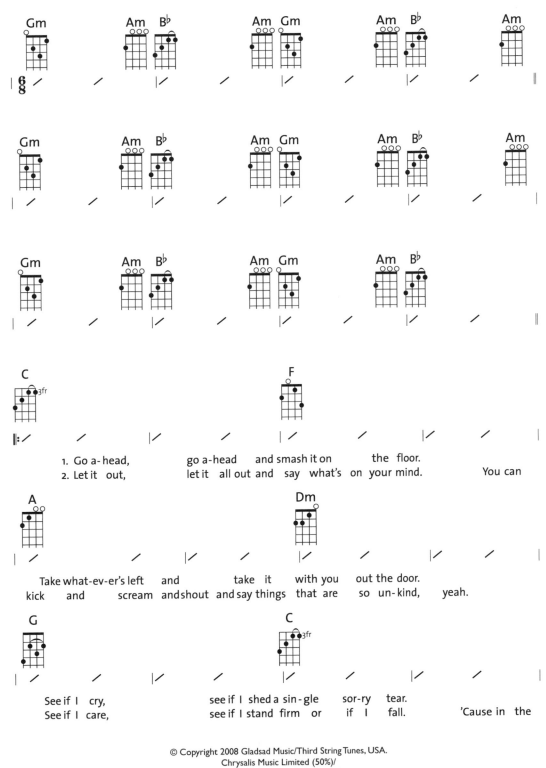

1. Go a-head,   go a-head   and smash it on   the floor.
2. Let it out,   let it all out and say what's on your mind.   You can

Take what-ev-er's left   and   take it   with you   out the door.
kick   and   scream andshout and say things that are   so un-kind,   yeah.

See if I cry,   see if I shed a sin-gle   sor-ry   tear.
See if I care,   see if I stand firm or   if I   fall.   'Cause in the

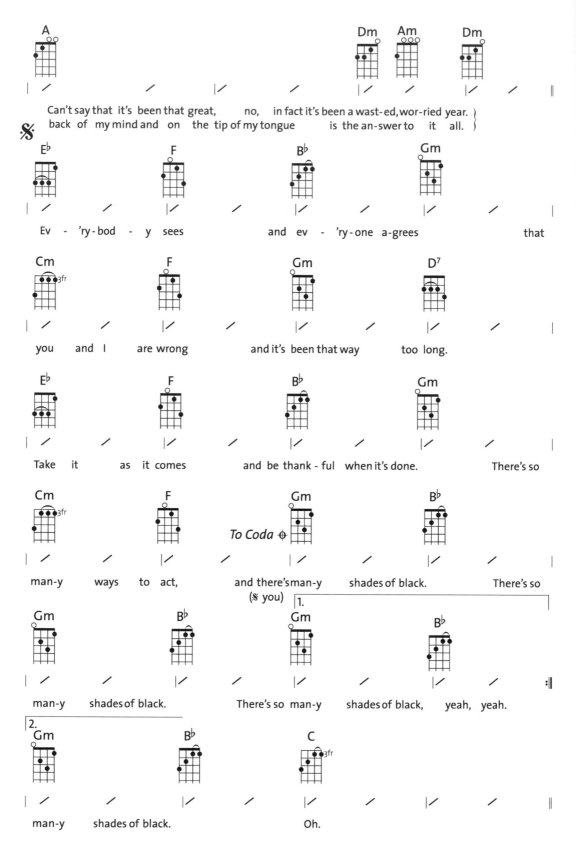

A   Dm   Am   Dm

Can't say that it's been that great,   no,   in fact it's been a wast-ed, wor-ried year.)
back of my mind and on the tip of my tongue   is the an-swer to it all.)

E♭   F   B♭   Gm

Ev - 'ry-bod - y sees   and ev - 'ry-one a-grees   that

Cm   F   Gm   D⁷

you   and I   are wrong   and it's been that way   too long.

E♭   F   B♭   Gm

Take it   as it comes   and be thank - ful when it's done.   There's so

Cm   F   Gm   B♭

To Coda ⊕

man-y   ways   to act,   and there's man-y   shades of black.   There's so

(% you) |1.

Gm   B♭   Gm   B♭

man-y   shades of black.   There's so man-y   shades of black,   yeah,   yeah.

|2.

Gm   B♭   C

man-y   shades of black.   Oh.

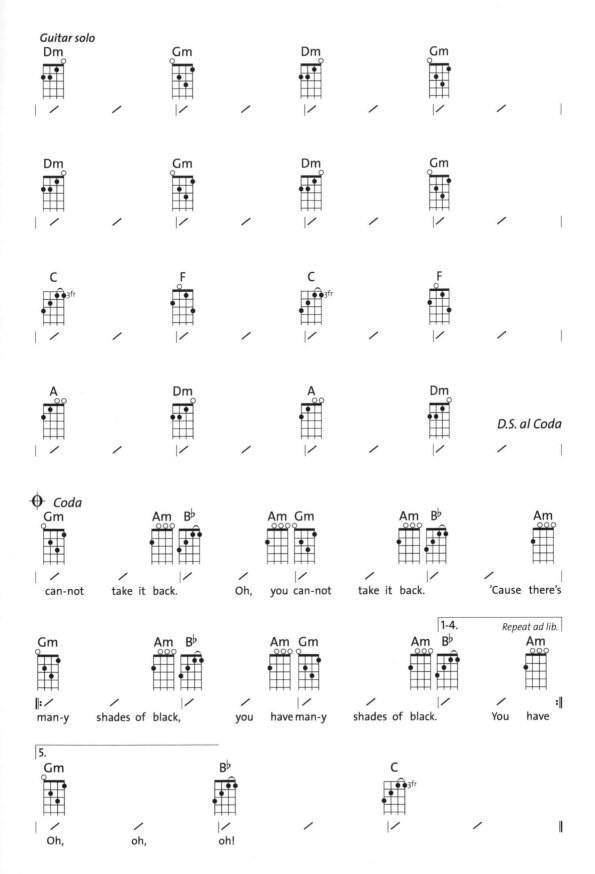

Guitar solo

Dm · Gm · Dm · Gm ·

Dm · Gm · Dm · Gm ·

C · F · C · F ·

A · Dm · A · Dm ·

D.S. al Coda

Coda

Gm · Am B♭ · Am Gm · Am B♭ · Am

can-not take it back. Oh, you can-not take it back. 'Cause there's

Gm · Am B♭ · Am Gm · Am B♭ · Am

1-4. *Repeat ad lib.*

man-y shades of black, you have man-y shades of black. You have

5.

Gm · B♭ · C ·

Oh, oh, oh!

35

My Same

Words & Music by Adele Adkins

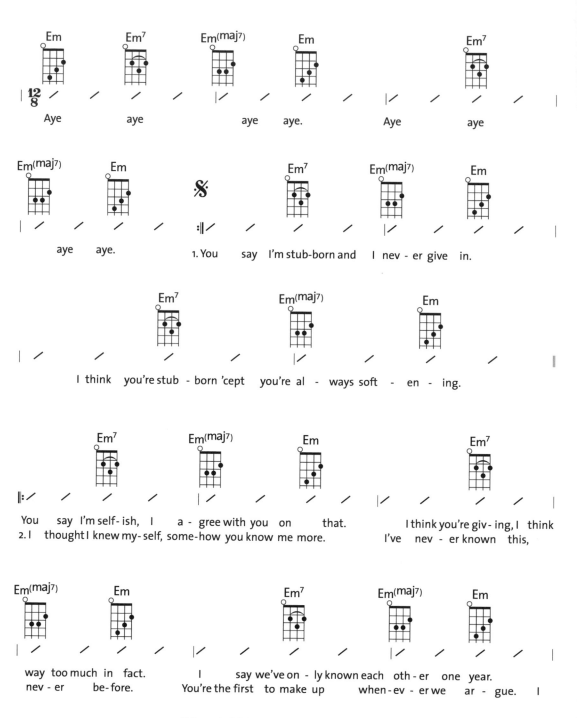

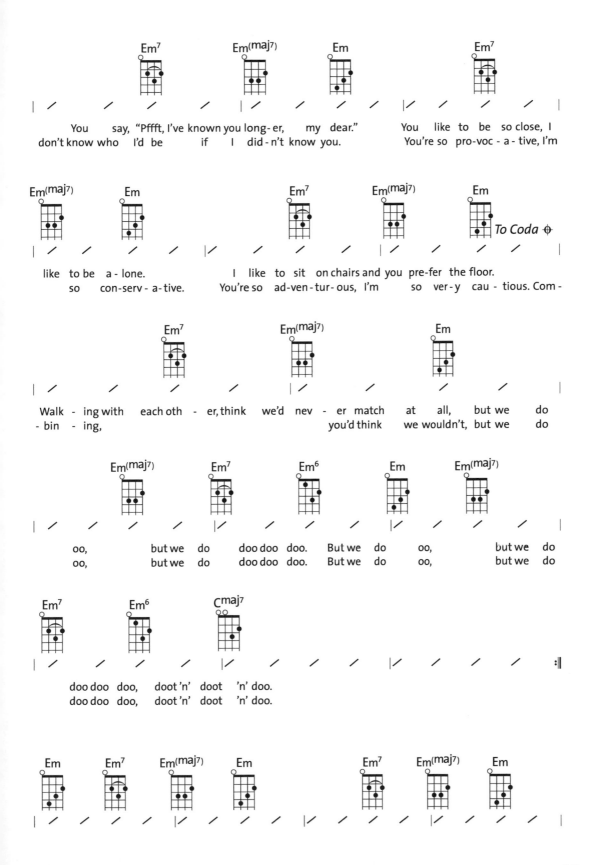

You say, "Pffft, I've known you long-er, my dear." You like to be so close, I
don't know who I'd be if I did-n't know you. You're so pro-voc-a-tive, I'm

To Coda ⊕

like to be a-lone. I like to sit on chairs and you pre-fer the floor.
so con-serv-a-tive. You're so ad-ven-tur-ous, I'm so ver-y cau-tious. Com-

Walk-ing with each oth-er, think we'd nev-er match at all, but we do
-bin-ing, you'd think we wouldn't, but we do

oo, but we do doo doo doo. But we do oo, but we do
oo, but we do doo doo doo. But we do oo, but we do

doo doo doo, doot 'n' doot 'n' doo.
doo doo doo, doot 'n' doot 'n' doo.

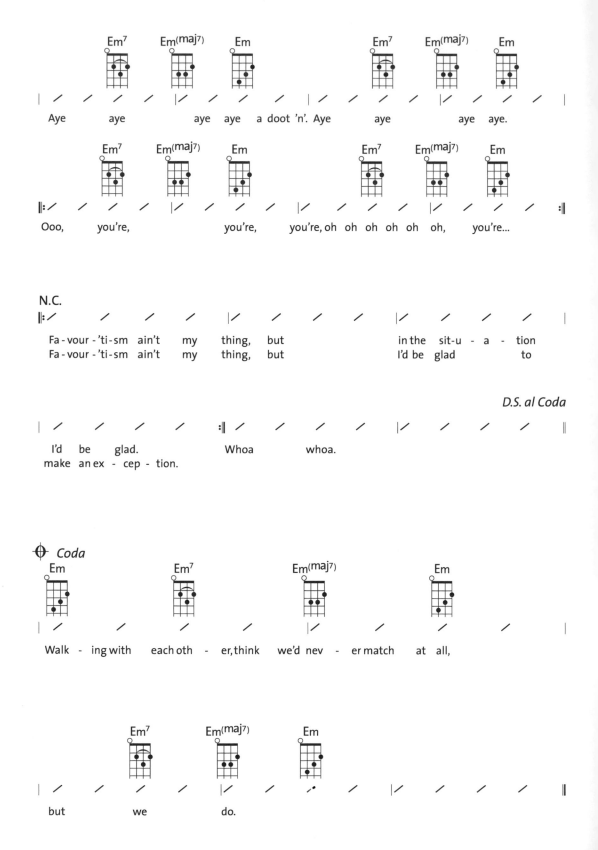

Em⁷ Em(maj7) Em   Em⁷ Em(maj7) Em

| / / / / | / / / / | / / / / | / / / / |

Aye   aye   aye aye a doot 'n'. Aye   aye   aye aye.

Em⁷ Em(maj7) Em   Em⁷ Em(maj7) Em

‖: / / / / | / / / / | / / / / | / / / / :‖

Ooo,   you're,   you're,   you're, oh oh oh oh oh oh,   you're...

N.C.

‖: / / / / | / / / / | / / / / | / / / / |

Fa - vour - 'ti-sm ain't   my   thing, but   in the sit-u - a - tion
Fa - vour - 'ti-sm ain't   my   thing, but   I'd be glad   to

D.S. al Coda

| / / / / :‖ / / / / | / / / / ‖

I'd   be   glad.   Whoa   whoa.
make an ex - cep - tion.

Coda

Em   Em⁷   Em(maj7)   Em

| / / / / | / / / / |

Walk - ing with   each oth - er, think   we'd nev - er match   at all,

Em⁷ Em(maj7) Em

| / / / / | / / / / | / / / / ‖

but   we   do.

38

Set Fire To The Rain

Words & Music by Fraser Smith & Adele Adkins

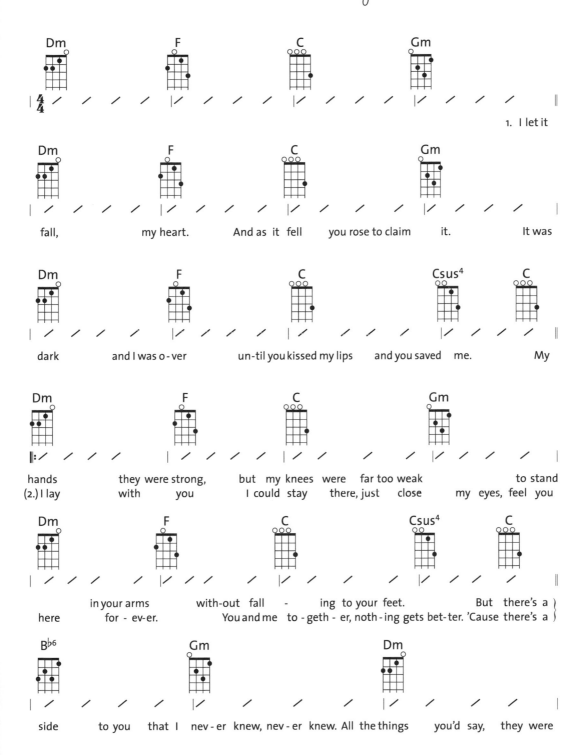

1. I let it
fall,   my heart.   And as it fell   you rose to claim   it.   It was

dark   and I was o-ver   un-til you kissed my lips   and you saved   me.   My

hands   they were strong,   but my knees were   far too weak   to stand
(2.) I lay   with   you   I could stay   there, just   close   my eyes, feel you

                in your arms   with-out fall - ing to your feet.   But there's a)
here   for - ev-er.   You and me to - geth - er, noth - ing gets bet - ter. 'Cause there's a)

side   to you   that I   nev - er knew, nev - er knew. All the things   you'd say,   they were

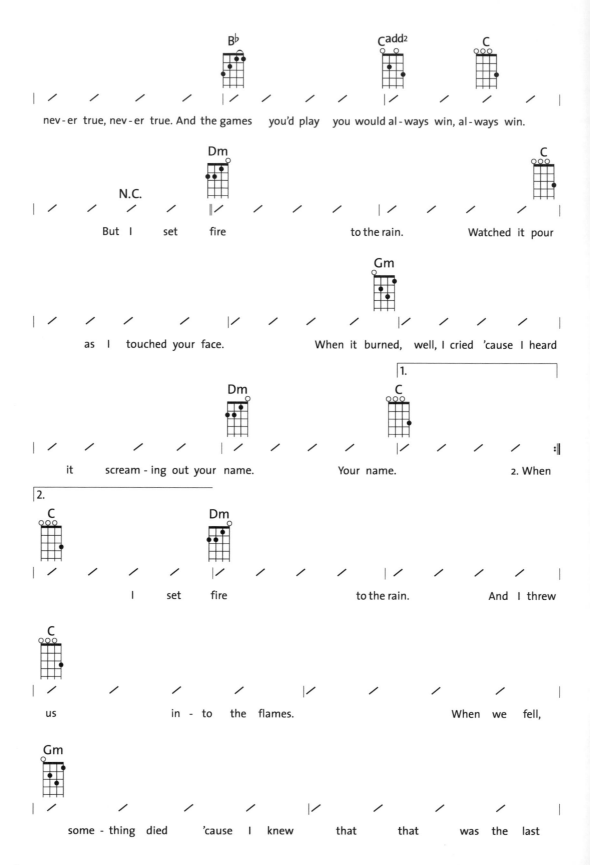

| / / / / | / / / / | / / / / |
nev-er true, nev-er true. And the games   you'd play   you would al-ways win, al-ways win.

| / / / / | / / / / | / / / / |
But I   set   fire   to the rain.   Watched it pour

| / / / / | / / / / | / / / / |
as I   touched your face.   When it burned,   well, I cried 'cause I heard

1.
| / / / / | / / / / | / / / / :|
it   scream-ing out your name.   Your name.   2. When

2.
| / / / / | / / / / | / / / / |
I   set   fire   to the rain.   And I threw

| / / / / | / / / / | / / / / |
us   in-to   the flames.   When we fell,

| / / / / | / / / / | / / / / |
some-thing died   'cause I   knew   that   that   was the last

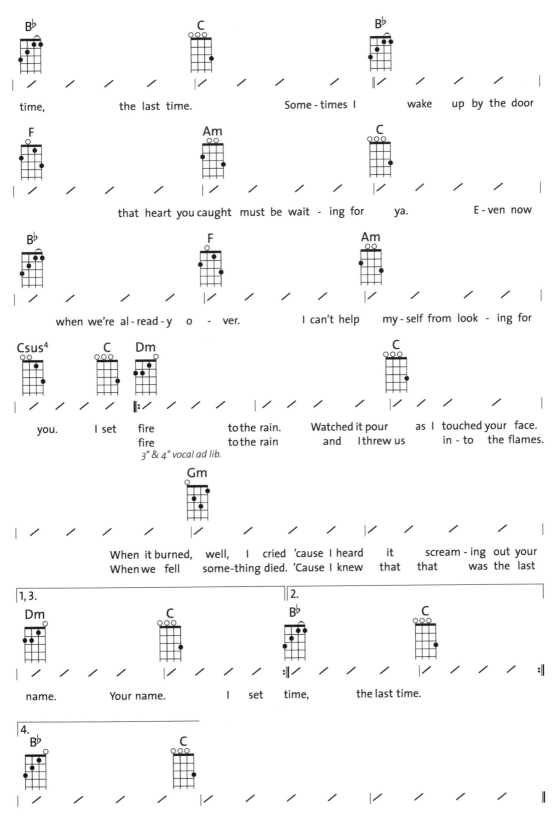

B♭				C				B♭				

time,   the last time.   Some - times I   wake   up by the door

F				Am				C				

that heart you caught must be wait - ing for   ya.   E - ven now

B♭				F				Am				

when we're al - read - y   o - ver.   I can't help   my - self from look - ing for

Csus⁴		C	Dm							C		

you.   I set   fire   to the rain.   Watched it pour   as I touched your face.
      fire   to the rain   and I threw us   in - to   the flames.

3° & 4° vocal ad lib.

				Gm								

When it burned,   well,   I cried 'cause I heard   it   scream - ing out your
When we fell   some - thing died. 'Cause I knew   that   that   was the last

1, 3.

Dm				C				**2.** B♭				C

name.   Your name.   I set   time,   the last time.

4.

B♭				C								

Rolling In The Deep

Words & Music by Adele Adkins & Paul Epworth

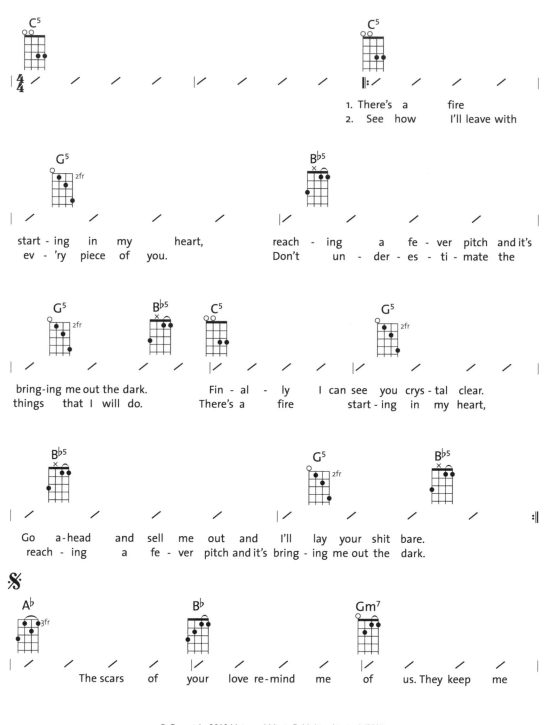

1. There's a fire
2. See how I'll leave with

start - ing in my heart, reach - ing a fe - ver pitch and it's
ev - 'ry piece of you. Don't un - der - es - ti - mate the

bring-ing me out the dark. Fin - al - ly I can see you crys - tal clear.
things that I will do. There's a fire start - ing in my heart,

Go a-head and sell me out and I'll lay your shit bare.
reach - ing a fe - ver pitch and it's bring - ing me out the dark.

The scars of your love re-mind me of us. They keep me

A♭

| / | / | / | / || / | / | / | / | |
think - ing that we al - most had it all. The scars of

B♭   Gm

| / | / | / || / | / | / | / | |
your love, they leave me breath - less. I can't help

G   Cm   B♭

| / | / | / | / ‖ / | / | / || / | / | / | / | |
feel-ing we could have had it all. Roll-ing in the

A♭maj⁷   B♭   Cm

| / | / | / | / || / | / | / || / | / | / | / | |
deep. You had my heart and soul 'side of your hand.

B♭   A♭maj⁷   *To Coda* ⊕   B♭

| / | / | / | / || / | / | / || / | / | / | / ‖
And you played it to the beat.

C⁵   G⁵   B♭5

| / | / | / | / || / | / | / || / | / | / | |
3. Ba - by, I have no sto - ry to be told. But I've heard one on you now I'm

G⁵   B♭5   C⁵   G⁵

| / | / | / | / || / | / | / || / | / | / | |
gon-na make your head burn. Think of me in the depths of your des - pair.

43

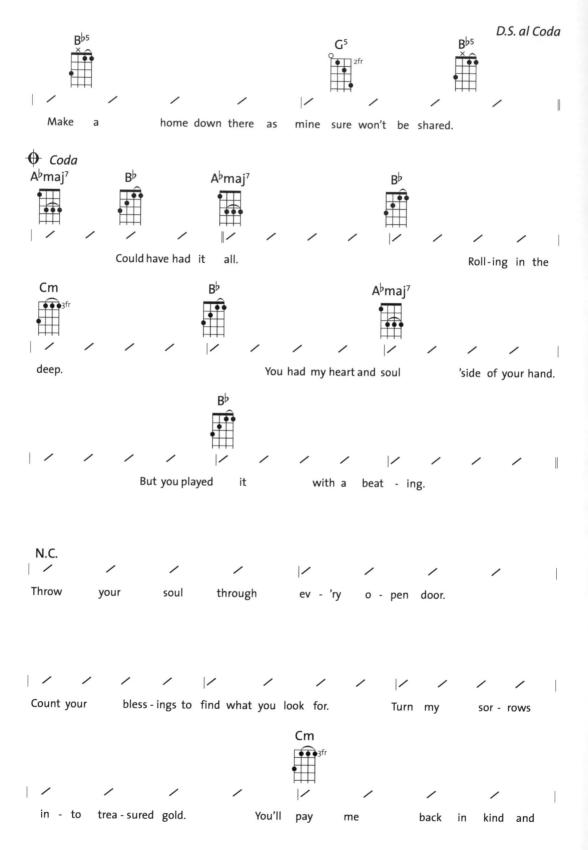

B♭5

G5
2fr

B♭5

Make a home down there as mine sure won't be shared.

Coda
A♭maj7   B♭   A♭maj7   B♭

Could have had it all.   Roll-ing in the

Cm
3fr   B♭   A♭maj7

deep.   You had my heart and soul   'side of your hand.

B♭

But you played it   with a beat - ing.

N.C.

Throw your soul through ev - 'ry o - pen door.

Count your bless - ings to find what you look for. Turn my sor - rows

Cm
3fr

in - to trea - sured gold. You'll pay me back in kind and

44

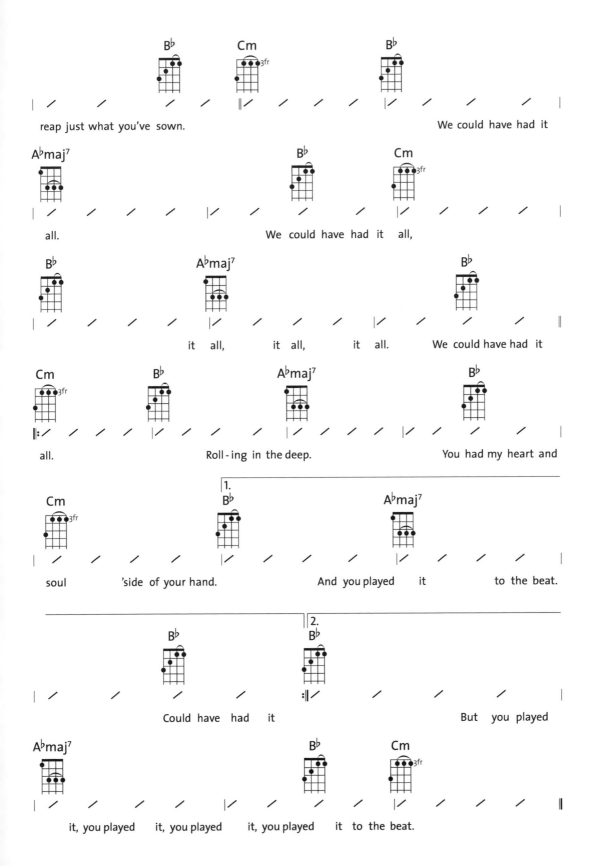

B♭   Cm   B♭

| /   / | /   / || /   /   / | /   /   / |

reap just what you've sown.   We could have had it

A♭maj⁷   B♭   Cm

| /   /   /   / | /   /   / | /   /   / |

all.   We could have had it   all,

B♭   A♭maj⁷   B♭

| /   /   /   / | /   /   / | /   /   / ||

it all,   it all,   it all.   We could have had it

Cm   B♭   A♭maj⁷   B♭

||: /   /   / | /   /   / | /   /   / | /   /   / |

all.   Roll-ing in the deep.   You had my heart and

1.

Cm   B♭   A♭maj⁷

| /   /   /   / | /   /   / | /   /   / |

soul   'side of your hand.   And you played   it   to the beat.

2.

B♭   B♭

| /   /   /   /   :|| /   /   /   / |

Could have had it   But you played

A♭maj⁷   B♭   Cm

| /   /   /   / | /   /   / | /   /   / ||

it, you played   it, you played   it, you played   it to the beat.

Someone Like You

Words & Music by Adele Adkins & Daniel Wilson

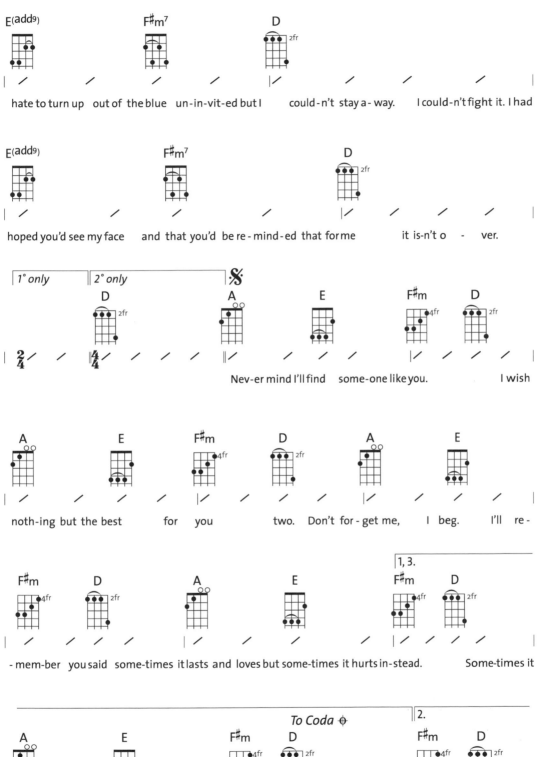

E(add9)　　　　　　　　F#m7　　　　　　　D

hate to turn up out of the blue un-in-vit-ed but I　could-n't stay a - way.　I could-n't fight it. I had

E(add9)　　　　　　　　F#m7　　　　　　　D

hoped you'd see my face　and that you'd be re - mind-ed that for me　it is-n't o - ver.

1° only　　2° only　　　　　　§
　　　　　D　　　　A　　　E　　　F#m　D

Nev-er mind I'll find　some-one like you.　　I wish

A　　　E　　　F#m　D　　　A　　　E

noth-ing but the best　for　you　two. Don't for - get me,　I beg.　I'll re -

1, 3.
F#m　D　　　A　　　E　　　F#m　D

- mem-ber you said some-times it lasts and loves but some-times it hurts in-stead.　Some-times it

To Coda ⊕　　　　　2.
A　　　E　　　F#m　D　　　F#m　D

lasts and loves　but some-times it hurts in-stead,　yeah.　- stead.

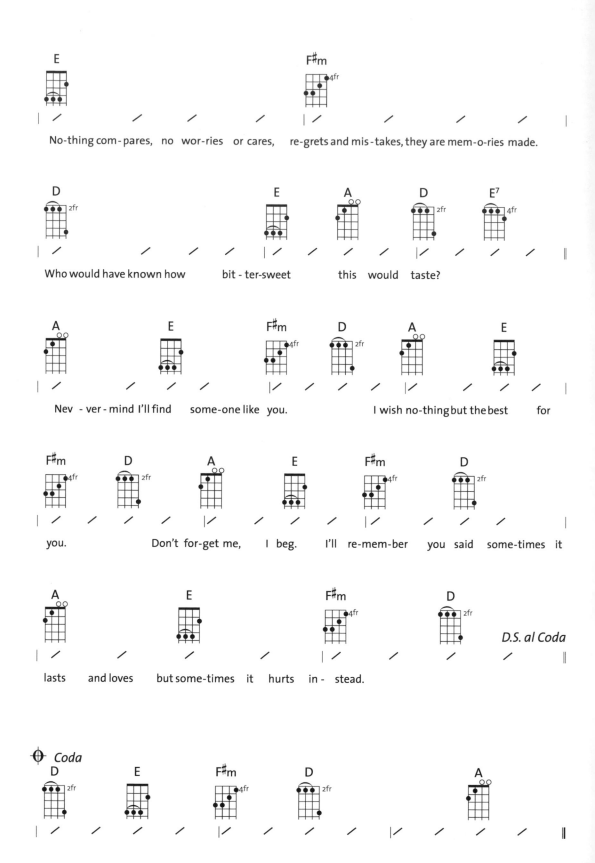

No-thing com-pares, no wor-ries or cares, re-grets and mis-takes, they are mem-o-ries made.

Who would have known how bit - ter-sweet this would taste?

Nev - ver - mind I'll find some-one like you. I wish no-thing but the best for

you. Don't for-get me, I beg. I'll re-mem-ber you said some-times it

lasts and loves but some-times it hurts in - stead.

D.S. al Coda

Coda